CHECKERBOARD BIOGRAPHY LIBRARY

U.S. PRESIDENTS

The
United States Presidents

JAMES BUCHANAN

ABDO Publishing Company

Megan M. Gunderson

visit us at
www.abdopublishing.com

Published by ABDO Publishing Company, 8000 West 78th Street, Edina, Minnesota 55439.
Copyright © 2009 by Abdo Consulting Group, Inc. International copyrights reserved in all
countries. No part of this book may be reproduced in any form without written permission from the
publisher. The Checkerboard Library™ is a trademark and logo of ABDO Publishing Company.

Printed in the United States.

Cover Photo: Getty Images
Interior Photos: Alamy pp. 23, 26, 29; Corbis pp. 5, 15, 27; Getty Images p. 28; iStockphoto p. 32;
     Library of Congress pp. 13, 14, 16, 17, 18, 20, 21, 24, 25; North Wind p. 9; Picture History
     pp. 11, 19

Editor: Heidi M.D. Elston
Art Direction & Cover Design: Neil Klinepier
Interior Design: Neil Klinepier

Library of Congress Cataloging-in-Publication Data

Gunderson, Megan M., 1981-
  James Buchanan / Megan M. Gunderson.
     p. cm. -- (The United States presidents)
  Includes index.
  ISBN 978-1-60453-442-9
  1. Buchanan, James, 1791-1868--Juvenile literature. 2. Presidents--United States--Biography--
Juvenile literature. I. Title.

  E437.G86 2009
  973.6'8092--dc22
  [B]
                                        2008030958

Contents

JAMES BUCHANAN

James Buchanan served as the fifteenth U.S. president. When he took office in 1857, he was nearly 66 years old. Buchanan had already worked in politics for more than 40 years.

Buchanan had a respected political career. He was a member of the Pennsylvania House of Representatives. Buchanan also served in the U.S. House of Representatives and the U.S. Senate. He was minister to Russia and to Great Britain. Buchanan also served as **secretary of state**.

As president, Buchanan faced a difficult time in the nation's history. The Northern and Southern states were arguing over slavery. The country was about to split apart.

President Buchanan tried to keep the country united. However, the slavery problem proved too difficult to fix. Before his term ended, several Southern states left the Union.

Buchanan disagreed with this action. Yet he could find no way to stop it. Soon after Buchanan left the White House, the American **Civil War** began.

TIMELINE

1791 - On April 23, James Buchanan was born in Cove Gap, Pennsylvania.

1809 - Buchanan graduated from Dickinson College in Carlisle, Pennsylvania.

1812 - Buchanan became a lawyer.

1814 - Buchanan's political career began in the Pennsylvania House of Representatives.

1821 - Buchanan began serving in the U.S. House of Representatives.

1830s - Buchanan served as minister to Russia.

1834 - Buchanan began serving in the U.S. Senate.

1845 - Under President James K. Polk, Buchanan became secretary of state.

1849 - Buchanan retired as secretary of state and moved to Wheatland.

1853 - President Franklin Pierce appointed Buchanan minister to Great Britain.

1854 - Buchanan signed the Ostend Manifesto.

1857 - Buchanan became the fifteenth U.S. president; he supported the Dred Scott decision.

1859 - John Brown led a rebellion at Harpers Ferry.

1861 - Buchanan retired to Wheatland; the American Civil War began.

1866 - *Mr. Buchanan's Administration on the Eve of the Rebellion* was published.

1868 - On June 1, James Buchanan died.

DID YOU KNOW?

James Buchanan's nickname was "Old Buck."

Buchanan is the only U.S. president who was born in the state of Pennsylvania.

President Buchanan was his niece Harriet Lane's guardian. She accompanied him to Great Britain while he was minister there. Then, she served as White House hostess for her unmarried uncle. She became very popular in Washington, D.C.

John C. Breckinridge took office at age 36. He is the youngest U.S. vice president in American history.

YOUNG JAMES

James Buchanan was born in Cove Gap, Pennsylvania, on April 23, 1791. His parents were James and Elizabeth Speer Buchanan. James was the second of their 11 children.

James's father was an Irish **immigrant**. He was a successful storekeeper and landowner. He taught James important business skills. Elizabeth taught James to love books and his country.

At school in nearby Mercersburg, Pennsylvania, James studied Latin and Greek. When he was only 16, James entered Dickinson College in Carlisle, Pennsylvania. He graduated in 1809.

James then studied law in Lancaster, Pennsylvania. In 1812, he became a lawyer. James was smart and worked hard. He quickly became successful.

FAST FACTS

BORN - April 23, 1791

WIFE - Never married

CHILDREN - None

POLITICAL PARTY - Democrat

AGE AT INAUGURATION - 65

YEARS SERVED - 1857–1861

VICE PRESIDENT - John C. Breckinridge

DIED - June 1, 1868, age 77

Dickinson College is named for Pennsylvania governor John Dickinson.

During this time, James briefly served in the **War of 1812**. He helped defend Baltimore, Maryland. Soon afterward, he began his career in politics.

POLITICS AND TRAGEDY

Buchanan's political career began in the Pennsylvania House of Representatives. At the time he was elected, Buchanan was a **Federalist**. He served from 1814 to 1816.

In 1819, Buchanan became engaged to Ann Caroline Coleman. Rumors and arguments led to the end of their engagement. Soon after, Ann died. Buchanan was heartbroken and never married. He remains the nation's only unmarried president.

Buchanan was elected to the U.S. House of Representatives in 1820. He served five terms from 1821 to 1831. There, he became chairman of the House Committee on the **Judiciary**.

As chairman, Buchanan served as **prosecutor** in an 1831 **impeachment** trial. James H. Peck was on trial. Peck was a U.S. district court judge in Missouri.

Missouri lawyer Luke Lawless had spoken out against Peck in a newspaper article. In it, he criticized several of Peck's court decisions.

Peck had sent Lawless to jail. He had also stopped Lawless from practicing law for 18 months. Buchanan argued that Peck had misused his powers as a judge. However, the U.S. Senate found Peck innocent.

Ann Coleman's family was upset with Buchanan after her death. They did not let him attend her funeral.

SERVING HIS COUNTRY

In the early 1830s, President Andrew Jackson made Buchanan minister to Russia. As minister, Buchanan arranged the first trade treaty between Russia and the United States.

After returning from Russia, Buchanan was elected to the U.S. Senate. He worked there from 1834 to 1845. Senator Buchanan served as chairman of the Committee on Foreign Relations. This group handles relations between the United States and other countries.

Senator Buchanan was also chairman of another committee. It worked toward ending the slave trade in the District of Columbia.

As part of this group, Buchanan defeated a proposed gag rule. Gag rules prevented people from introducing **petitions** against slavery in the Senate. This would have kept laws against slavery from being passed.

Buchanan gained valuable experience working in foreign countries. This helped prepare him for being secretary of state and president.

James K. Polk was president from 1845 to 1849.

In 1845, Buchanan became President James K. Polk's **secretary of state**. At the time, the United States had problems to settle with other countries. As secretary, Buchanan helped settle a border disagreement with England over the Oregon Territory.

Buchanan also tried to settle a border argument with Mexico. But, his attempts failed. The disagreement led to the Mexican War. The United States and Mexico fought the war from 1846 to 1848.

In 1846, Pennsylvania congressman David Wilmot proposed the Wilmot Proviso. It would have banned slavery in any territory gained from Mexico.

Buchanan morally opposed slavery. However, he believed slavery was legal according to the U.S. **Constitution**. Buchanan believed in always following the law, even if it was difficult. So, he opposed Wilmot's ideas.

Done at Washington the fifteenth day of June, in the year of our Lord one thousand eight hundred and forty-six.

James Buchanan

Richard L. Pakenham.

In 1846, Buchanan signed the treaty that established Oregon's northern border.

The country continued to argue about slavery. So, Kentucky senator Henry Clay proposed a group of new laws. These became the Compromise of 1850. Buchanan supported this.

Part of the Compromise of 1850 attempted to keep the same number of free and slave states in the Senate. Another part was the Fugitive Slave Law. This law stated rules for returning runaway slaves to their owners.

A New Position

President Polk's term ended in 1849. At that time, Buchanan retired as **secretary of state**. He moved to a new house near Lancaster. It was called Wheatland.

There, Buchanan planned his campaign for the 1852 election. He had joined the **Democratic** Party when the **Federalist** Party broke up. Now, Buchanan hoped the Democrats would nominate him for president.

Buchanan had a lot of political experience. So, many Democrats believed he would make a good candidate. Yet they nominated Franklin Pierce for president.

Buchanan supported Pierce during the campaign. Pierce won the 1852 election. Then in 1853, he made Buchanan minister to Great Britain.

Franklin Pierce served one term as president, from 1853 to 1857.

16

While minister, Buchanan became involved in Pierce's efforts to gain Cuba. In 1854, Buchanan signed the Ostend Manifesto. It recommended that the United States seize Cuba from Spain.

Many Americans disagreed with this plan. Others believed gaining Cuba was a good idea. The United States would get more land. And, many Southerners wanted Cuba to become a slave state. In the end, the government did not take over Cuba.

Signing the Ostend Manifesto earned Buchanan support in the South. This helped him win the presidential nomination in 1856.

THE ELECTION OF 1856

In 1856, the **Democrats** nominated Buchanan to run for president. His **running mate** was John C. Breckinridge of Kentucky. Former president Millard Fillmore ran as the **American** Party candidate. John C. Frémont ran for the new **Republican** Party.

The Republican Party had formed in 1854. It opposed the spread of slavery. Many people who were against slavery joined this new party. This included some Democrats.

Still, Buchanan and Breckinridge won the election. They received fewer than half

John C. Breckinridge

SUPREME COURT APPOINTMENT

NATHAN CLIFFORD - 1858

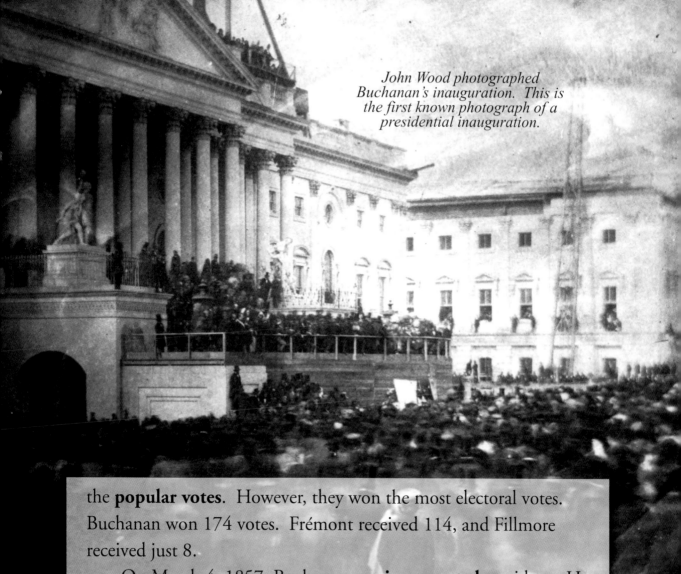

John Wood photographed Buchanan's inauguration. This is the first known photograph of a presidential inauguration.

the **popular votes**. However, they won the most electoral votes. Buchanan won 174 votes. Frémont received 114, and Fillmore received just 8.

On March 4, 1857, Buchanan was **inaugurated** president. He became president as the slavery **debate** reached its peak. Still, Buchanan hoped the problem would be settled in court.

DRED SCOTT

Two days after Buchanan took office, the U.S. **Supreme Court** decided the *Dred Scott* case. Most people hoped this important case would settle the slavery issue.

Dred Scott was a Missouri slave. He had once traveled with his owner to Illinois and the Wisconsin Territory. After returning to Missouri, Scott **sued** for his freedom. He had lived in a free state and a free territory. So, Scott argued he was a free man. On March 6, 1857, the Supreme Court ruled against Scott. **Chief Justice** Roger B. Taney stated that slaves were property. He

Dred Scott

argued that a person could not be denied his property. And, he said that slaves had no right to **sue** in court.

President Buchanan supported the **Supreme Court**'s decision. He hoped the slavery problem was settled once and for all. But the *Dred Scott* decision was hated throughout the North. There, support for the **Republican** Party continued to grow.

Like Buchanan, Roger B. Taney attended Dickinson College.

BLEEDING KANSAS

President Buchanan's troubles continued. The Kansas Territory had been involved in the Kansas-Nebraska Act in 1854. It stated that voters would decide if they wanted slavery. This would happen when Kansas adopted a state **constitution**.

The slavery issue caused bitter battles throughout the territory. The conflict became known as "Bleeding Kansas."

When Buchanan took office, Kansas had two governments. The government in Lecompton supported slavery. The government in Topeka was against it.

Most people in Kansas were against slavery. But in 1857, those against slavery refused to register to vote. So, only those who favored slavery were elected to write the state constitution. They passed the Lecompton Constitution, which allowed slavery.

Republicans and Northern **Democrats** were angry. They felt Kansas should be a free state. Buchanan agreed. But he still supported the Lecompton Constitution. That is because it had been created legally.

The Lecompton Constitution was signed at Constitution Hall in Lecompton, Kansas.

The Senate approved the Lecompton **Constitution**. However, the House did not. As a replacement, Indiana representative William H. English created the English Bill.

The English Bill would allow Kansas to be a slave state. But, it reduced the amount of land Kansas would get from the government. So on August 2, 1858, people in Kansas voted again. This time, they rejected the constitution. Kansas eventually joined the United States as a free state in January 1861.

HARPERS FERRY

Buchanan's slavery problems did not end there. **Abolitionist** John Brown was leading a **rebellion** against slavery. On October 16, 1859, Brown seized the U.S. arsenal at Harpers Ferry. This weapons storage area was in present-day West Virginia.

Brown hoped escaped slaves would join him in the fight against slavery. However, national troops arrived at Harpers Ferry on October 17. They fought Brown and his followers. Seventeen people died. Brown was taken prisoner and found guilty of treason. He was hanged on December 2.

John Brown

This event further divided the North and the South. Buchanan had trouble leading a divided nation. Northerners were upset that Buchanan defended slavery and the South. It was certain the **Democrats** would not nominate Buchanan for a second term.

Two of John Brown's sons died in the fighting at Harpers Ferry.

LAST DAYS IN OFFICE

During Buchanan's last four months in office, seven Southern states **seceded**. South Carolina, Mississippi, Florida, Alabama, Georgia, Louisiana, and Texas left the Union. They started their own country called the Confederate States of America.

Buchanan was against these actions. But he was torn. He felt there was no legal way to stop the states. However, he also felt they had no legal right to separate.

In January 1861, Buchanan sent supplies to Fort Sumter in South Carolina. This U.S. fort was now in Confederate territory. Confederate forces surrounded the fort. They forced the supply ships to turn back. Before Buchanan could try to help the fort again, his term ended.

Confederate forces fired on Fort Sumter on April 12, 1861. This sparked the American Civil War.

26

PRESIDENT BUCHANAN'S CABINET

MARCH 4, 1857–MARCH 4, 1861

- **STATE –** Lewis Cass
  Jeremiah S. Black (from December 17, 1860)
- **TREASURY –** Howell Cobb
  Philip F. Thomas (from December 12, 1860)
  John A. Dix (from January 15, 1861)

- **WAR –** John B. Floyd
- **NAVY –** Isaac Toucey
- **ATTORNEY GENERAL –** Jeremiah S. Black
  Edwin M. Stanton (from December 22, 1860)
- **INTERIOR –** Jacob Thompson

Buchanan (center) *and his cabinet*

AFTER THE WHITE HOUSE

Buchanan died at Wheatland and was buried in Lancaster, Pennsylvania.

On March 4, 1861, Buchanan's long political career ended. That day, **Republican** Abraham Lincoln became the sixteenth U.S. president.

Buchanan then retired to Wheatland. Soon after, the American **Civil War** began. During the war, Buchanan strongly supported the Union.

At the time, many people blamed Buchanan for not preventing the war.

28

So in 1866, he published *Mr. Buchanan's Administration on the Eve of the **Rebellion***. The work defended his actions during his time in office.

James Buchanan died on June 1, 1868. Today, he is praised for delaying the war in the hopes of peace. Many people believe he did what he could against impossible odds.

OFFICE OF THE PRESIDENT

BRANCHES OF GOVERNMENT

The U.S. government is divided into three branches. They are the executive, legislative, and judicial branches. This division is called a separation of powers. Each branch has some power over the others. This is called a system of checks and balances.

EXECUTIVE BRANCH

The executive branch enforces laws. It is made up of the president, the vice president, and the president's cabinet. The president represents the United States around the world. He or she oversees relations with other countries and signs treaties. The president signs bills into law and appoints officials and federal judges. He or she also leads the military and manages government workers.

LEGISLATIVE BRANCH

The legislative branch makes laws, maintains the military, and regulates trade. It also has the power to declare war. This branch consists of the Senate and the House of Representatives. Together, these two houses make up Congress. Each state has two senators. A state's population determines the number of representatives it has.

JUDICIAL BRANCH

The judicial branch interprets laws. It consists of district courts, courts of appeals, and the Supreme Court. District courts try cases. If a person disagrees with a trial's outcome, he or she may appeal. If the courts of appeals support the ruling, a person may appeal to the Supreme Court. The Supreme Court also makes sure that laws follow the U.S. Constitution.

QUALIFICATIONS FOR OFFICE

To be president, a person must meet three requirements. A candidate must be at least 35 years old and a natural-born U.S. citizen. He or she must also have lived in the United States for at least 14 years.

ELECTORAL COLLEGE

The U.S. presidential election is an indirect election. Voters from each state choose electors to represent them in the Electoral College. The number of electors from each state is based on population. Each elector has one electoral vote. Electors are pledged to cast their vote for the candidate who receives the highest number of popular votes in their state. A candidate must receive the majority of Electoral College votes to win.

TERM OF OFFICE

Each president may be elected to two four-year terms. Sometimes, a president may only be elected once. This happens if he or she served more than two years of the previous president's term.

The presidential election is held on the Tuesday after the first Monday in November. The president is sworn in on January 20 of the following year. At that time, he or she takes the oath of office:

I do solemnly swear (or affirm) that I will faithfully execute the office of President of the United States, and will to the best of my ability, preserve, protect and defend the Constitution of the United States.

LINE OF SUCCESSION

The Presidential Succession Act of 1947 defines who becomes president if the president cannot serve. The vice president is first in the line of succession. Next are the Speaker of the House and the President Pro Tempore of the Senate. If none of these individuals is able to serve, the office falls to the president's cabinet members. They would take office in the order in which each department was created:

Secretary of State

Secretary of the Treasury

Secretary of Defense

Attorney General

Secretary of the Interior

Secretary of Agriculture

Secretary of Commerce

Secretary of Labor

Secretary of Health and Human Services

Secretary of Housing and Urban Development

Secretary of Transportation

Secretary of Energy

Secretary of Education

Secretary of Veterans Affairs

Secretary of Homeland Security

BENEFITS

• While in office, the president receives a salary of $400,000 each year. He or she lives in the White House and has 24-hour Secret Service protection.

• The president may travel on a Boeing 747 jet called Air Force One. The airplane can accommodate 70 passengers. It has kitchens, a dining room, sleeping areas, and a conference room. It also has fully equipped offices with the latest communications systems. Air Force One can fly halfway around the world before needing to refuel. It can even refuel in flight!

• If the president wishes to travel by car, he or she uses Cadillac One. Cadillac One is a Cadillac Deville. It has been modified with heavy armor and communications systems. The president takes Cadillac One along when visiting other countries if secure transportation will be needed.

• The president also travels on a helicopter called Marine One. Like the presidential car, Marine One accompanies the president when traveling abroad if necessary.

• Sometimes, the president needs to get away and relax with family and friends. Camp David is the official presidential retreat. It is located in the cool, wooded mountains in Maryland. The U.S. Navy maintains the retreat, and the U.S. Marine Corps keeps it secure. The camp offers swimming, tennis, golf, and hiking.

• When the president leaves office, he or she receives Secret Service protection for ten more years. He or she also receives a yearly pension of $191,300 and funding for office space, supplies, and staff.

PRESIDENTS AND THEIR TERMS

PRESIDENT	PARTY	TOOK OFFICE	LEFT OFFICE	TERMS SERVED	VICE PRESIDENT
George Washington	None	April 30, 1789	March 4, 1797	Two	John Adams
John Adams	Federalist	March 4, 1797	March 4, 1801	One	Thomas Jefferson
Thomas Jefferson	Democratic-Republican	March 4, 1801	March 4, 1809	Two	Aaron Burr, George Clinton
James Madison	Democratic-Republican	March 4, 1809	March 4, 1817	Two	George Clinton, Elbridge Gerry
James Monroe	Democratic-Republican	March 4, 1817	March 4, 1825	Two	Daniel D. Tompkins
John Quincy Adams	Democratic-Republican	March 4, 1825	March 4, 1829	One	John C. Calhoun
Andrew Jackson	Democrat	March 4, 1829	March 4, 1837	Two	John C. Calhoun, Martin Van Buren
Martin Van Buren	Democrat	March 4, 1837	March 4, 1841	One	Richard M. Johnson
William H. Harrison	Whig	March 4, 1841	April 4, 1841	Died During First Term	John Tyler
John Tyler	Whig	April 6, 1841	March 4, 1845	Completed Harrison's Term	Office Vacant
James K. Polk	Democrat	March 4, 1845	March 4, 1849	One	George M. Dallas
Zachary Taylor	Whig	March 5, 1849	July 9, 1850	Died During First Term	Millard Fillmore

PRESIDENT	PARTY	TOOK OFFICE	LEFT OFFICE	TERMS SERVED	VICE PRESIDENT
Millard Fillmore	Whig	July 10, 1850	March 4, 1853	Completed Taylor's Term	Office Vacant
Franklin Pierce	Democrat	March 4, 1853	March 4, 1857	One	William R.D. King
James Buchanan	Democrat	March 4, 1857	March 4, 1861	One	John C. Breckinridge
Abraham Lincoln	Republican	March 4, 1861	April 15, 1865	Served One Term, Died During Second Term	Hannibal Hamlin, Andrew Johnson
Andrew Johnson	Democrat	April 15, 1865	March 4, 1869	Completed Lincoln's Second Term	Office Vacant
Ulysses S. Grant	Republican	March 4, 1869	March 4, 1877	Two	Schuyler Colfax, Henry Wilson
Rutherford B. Hayes	Republican	March 3, 1877	March 4, 1881	One	William A. Wheeler
James A. Garfield	Republican	March 4, 1881	September 19, 1881	Died During First Term	Chester Arthur
Chester Arthur	Republican	September 20, 1881	March 4, 1885	Completed Garfield's Term	Office Vacant
Grover Cleveland	Democrat	March 4, 1885	March 4, 1889	One	Thomas A. Hendricks
Benjamin Harrison	Republican	March 4, 1889	March 4, 1893	One	Levi P. Morton
Grover Cleveland	Democrat	March 4, 1893	March 4, 1897	One	Adlai E. Stevenson
William McKinley	Republican	March 4, 1897	September 14, 1901	Served One Term, Died During Second Term	Garret A. Hobart, Theodore Roosevelt

PRESIDENT	PARTY	TOOK OFFICE	LEFT OFFICE	TERMS SERVED	VICE PRESIDENT
Theodore Roosevelt	Republican	September 14, 1901	March 4, 1909	Completed McKinley's Second Term, Served One Term	Office Vacant, Charles Fairbanks
William Taft	Republican	March 4, 1909	March 4, 1913	One	James S. Sherman
Woodrow Wilson	Democrat	March 4, 1913	March 4, 1921	Two	Thomas R. Marshall
Warren G. Harding	Republican	March 4, 1921	August 2, 1923	Died During First Term	Calvin Coolidge
Calvin Coolidge	Republican	August 3, 1923	March 4, 1929	Completed Harding's Term, Served One Term	Office Vacant, Charles Dawes
Herbert Hoover	Republican	March 4, 1929	March 4, 1933	One	Charles Curtis
Franklin D. Roosevelt	Democrat	March 4, 1933	April 12, 1945	Served Three Terms, Died During Fourth Term	John Nance Garner, Henry A. Wallace, Harry S. Truman
Harry S. Truman	Democrat	April 12, 1945	January 20, 1953	Completed Roosevelt's Fourth Term, Served One Term	Office Vacant, Alben Barkley
Dwight D. Eisenhower	Republican	January 20, 1953	January 20, 1961	Two	Richard Nixon
John F. Kennedy	Democrat	January 20, 1961	November 22, 1963	Died During First Term	Lyndon B. Johnson
Lyndon B. Johnson	Democrat	November 22, 1963	January 20, 1969	Completed Kennedy's Term, Served One Term	Office Vacant, Hubert H. Humphrey
Richard Nixon	Republican	January 20, 1969	August 9, 1974	Completed First Term, Resigned During Second Term	Spiro T. Agnew, Gerald Ford

PRESIDENT	PARTY	TOOK OFFICE	LEFT OFFICE	TERMS SERVED	VICE PRESIDENT
Gerald Ford	Republican	August 9, 1974	January 20, 1977	Completed Nixon's Second Term	Nelson A. Rockefeller
Jimmy Carter	Democrat	January 20, 1977	January 20, 1981	One	Walter Mondale
Ronald Reagan	Republican	January 20, 1981	January 20, 1989	Two	George H.W. Bush
George H.W. Bush	Republican	January 20, 1989	January 20, 1993	One	Dan Quayle
Bill Clinton	Democrat	January 20, 1993	January 20, 2001	Two	Al Gore
George W. Bush	Republican	January 20, 2001	January 20, 2009	Two	Dick Cheney
Barack Obama	Democrat	January 20, 2009			Joe Biden

"We ought to do justice in a kindly spirit to all nations and require justice from them in return." James Buchanan

WRITE TO THE PRESIDENT

You may write to the president at:

**The White House
1600 Pennsylvania Avenue NW
Washington, DC 20500**

You may e-mail the president at:
comments@whitehouse.gov

GLOSSARY

abolitionist - a person who is against slavery.

American - a member of the American political party. During the 1850s, the American Party supported limiting the number of people who could move to the United States from other countries.

chief justice - the head judge of the U.S. Supreme Court.

civil war - a war between groups in the same country. The United States of America and the Confederate States of America fought a civil war from 1861 to 1865.

constitution - the laws that govern a country or a state. The U.S. Constitution is the laws that govern the United States.

debate - a contest in which two sides argue for or against something.

Democrat - a member of the Democratic political party. When James Buchanan was president, Democrats supported farmers and landowners.

Federalist - a member of the Federalist political party. During the early 1800s, Federalists believed in a strong national government.

immigrant - a person who immigrates. To immigrate is to enter another country to live.

impeach - to charge a public official with misconduct in office.

inaugurate (ih-NAW-gyuh-rayt) - to swear into a political office.

judiciary (joo-DIH-shee-ehr-ee) - the branch of a government in charge of courts and judges.

petition - a formal request to an organized group or a person of authority.

popular vote - the vote of the entire body of people with the right to vote.

prosecutor - a lawyer who argues to convict the person on trial.

rebellion - an armed resistance or a defiance of a government.

Republican - a member of the Republican political party. When James Buchanan was president, Republicans supported business and strong government.

running mate - a candidate running for a lower-rank position on an election ticket, especially the candidate for vice president.

secede - to break away from a group.

secretary of state - a member of the president's cabinet who handles relations with other countries.

sue - to bring a person or an organization to court.

Supreme Court - the highest, most powerful court in the United States.

War of 1812 - from 1812 to 1814. A war fought between the United States and Great Britain over shipping rights and the capture of U.S. soldiers.

WEB SITES

To learn more about James Buchanan, visit ABDO Publishing Company on the World Wide Web at **www.abdopublishing.com**. Web sites about James Buchanan are featured on our Book Links page. These links are routinely monitored and updated to provide the most current information available.

INDEX

J B BUCHANAN

Gunderson, Megan M.
James Buchanan

SOF

R4002310493

SOUTH FULTON BRANCH
Atlanta-Fulton Public Library